IN INCREDIBLY SIMPLE STEPS

MEDITATION FOR BEGINNERS

Jean R. Echols

Contents

1. Introduction — 1

2. Concentration in Mindfulness Vs. Concentration in Meditation — 15

3. Improve your breathing technique — 28

4. Calm Your Mind — 36

5. Educate yourself — 50

6. Make Meditation a Daily Routine — 58

Chapter One

Introduction

Meditation is a one-of-a-kind, all-encompassing method of training your mind to be calmer and more positive while pushing negativity away. Sitting cross-legged, closing your eyes, and chanting "ohm" isn't always necessary. Meditation can be done in various ways. While meditating, you must maintain physical silence in your surroundings as well.

Meditation should aid in the clearing of your mind of all unwanted thoughts. Maintaining good posture, remaining quiet, and focusing on your breathing are three important lessons you will learn while meditating. You'll learn to empty your mind of thoughts and emotions, as well as how to be more present and focused on the present moment. You'll feel more relaxed, and you'll be able to focus on each breath you take.

This simple act of meditation will assist you in escaping the anxiety and stress of daily life. While meditating, you are not required to think about the past or the future. The past has passed us by, and the future awaits us. Your present is the only aspect of your life over which you have control; however, most people find it extremely difficult to maintain their focus on the present.

This can be changed through meditation. Fighting your mind's natural proclivity to wander can be difficult at first. Slowly but steadily, you will master the art of concentration training.

The benefits of meditation have been well-documented for thousands of years. Meditation has flourished in cultures all over the world for centuries. Despite its reputation as a more eastern practice, meditation has gained popularity in the western world in recent years as a result of the numerous benefits it provides. Clearing one's mind rather than being filled with doubts can be an enlightening experience. To be effective, however, you must believe in the benefits of meditation.

Everyone can benefit from meditation. Modern life can be hectic and stressful, and it can be overwhelming at times. In general, our lives have become tense and exhausting. Regardless of whether they are wealthy or poor, successful or struggling, no one appears to be truly happy and satisfied with their lives.

Every day, meditate to find the strength to get through the day with a positive attitude. Meditation can assist you in coping with troubling and complex thoughts or feelings that have been bothering you. You can escape the monotony of daily life by practicing meditation. You will notice positive changes in yourself and feel better every time you meditate.

One of the most beneficial practices one can incorporate into their daily routine is meditation. As you will learn in this book, making meditation a habit will benefit you in numerous ways. It becomes a natural habit that provides numerous advantages over time. Meditation can be done in a variety of ways, and the results vary from person to person. Some techniques that work for others may not work for you, but after reading this book, you will have a variety of options from which to choose, allowing you to find the techniques that are right for you.

Part 1: A Step-By-Step Guide to Simple Meditations

Preparation for Meditation is the first step.

The first stage of the meditation process is to prepare for it. It is necessary to prepare for any type of meditation in order for it to be successful.

Stage Zero is frequently overlooked as an afterthought, and it is either skipped or incompletely completed. This is unfortunate because it reduces the effectiveness of meditation before it even starts.

You must create the proper conditions in order to achieve a specific result. According to Buddhists, if your goal is to achieve "x," you must first set up the conditions to achieve "x."

The importance of preparation is heavily emphasized by Buddhists. They believe that skipping this step will result in you not getting the desired results.

Both external and internal preparation are required for meditation. You want to create an environment that promotes a deep, meditative experience from the outside. Internally, you should focus on improving your posture, increasing your body awareness, and relaxing as much as possible. This preparation is necessary for a mind that is more calm, less stressed, and peaceful.

Here are some tips for getting the most out of your meditation by preparing your external and internal environments.

External actions should reflect your internal intent.

Mentally, you're emptying your mind of all useless, powerless human thoughts and reloading it with thoughts that align with your spiritual higher self.

Showering (to wash away your worries), brushing your teeth, or washing your hands and face are all physical ways to demonstrate your desire to purify your thoughts. Washing is a powerfully symbolic cleansing ritual that will leave you feeling renewed, refreshed, and clean. As you prepare to meditate, it can also have a hugely beneficial effect on your mood and overall mindset.

Establish a soothing environment.

Create a relaxing environment for your body and mind.

Dim the lights, light a candle, burn incense, arrange fresh flowers on the table, or listen to meditation music. Creating a meditation sanctuary will go a long way toward clearing your mind and allowing you to meditate in a deep, enjoyable, and enriching way.

To induce a meditative state, use the following techniques.

Read spiritual writings for 5 to 20 minutes. These can include anything from biblical God-centered books to spiritual healing materials to positive, encouraging words that nourish your soul and connect you with your Spirit. Consider the meaning of each sentence as you read. Make notes in a special journal for spiritual reflection.

Deeply inhale

Take between 5 and 10 slow, deep breaths when you feel your spiritual reading has brought you to a place of awareness and peace. Open your heart to God's peaceful, loving nature as you take a deep breath in (or the Universe). Allow the tension and frustrations in your subconscious mind to be released through your outward breath. Remove them from the situation. Now you can start your chosen meditation practice. With each full, deep breath, breathe from the diaphragm and feel your body relax.

Select your most convenient time.

In terms of the best time to meditate, there are no hard and fast rules. It is up to you and your schedule to decide what works best for you.

Some people prefer morning meditation because it helps them maintain a positive attitude throughout the day. Others prefer to meditate after work or school to help them unwind from the day's stresses.

Others prefer to meditate right before bedtime so that their subconscious minds can work on their goals while they sleep. Some people will struggle during this time because they are tired and can't sleep.

Select the most convenient time of day for you. It may take some trial and error to find your ideal time, but once you do, it will nourish your meditative practice for months or years to come.

Make yourself at ease and sit up straight.

To begin, dress in loose-fitting clothing that will not restrict or confine you. Make sure the area you've designated as your meditation sanctuary is warm enough for you to meditate comfortably.

Because the emotions and mental state you experience during meditation are ultimately attributable to the way you hold your body during meditation, the way you sit is critical. Even seemingly insignificant factors like the angle at which your chin is held can have an impact on your thoughts. As a result, one of the first things you should learn is how to sit correctly.

When it comes to preparing a suitable posture for meditation, there are two key principles to remember:

You should be at ease and relaxed in your posture. You must maintain an alert and aware posture.

You won't be able to meditate if you're feeling uneasy. You will not be able to enjoy meditation if you are unable to relax.

Sitting cross-legged on a meditation pillow might be a good option. If you aren't very flexible, however, you will most likely suffer as a result of this. Sit in a chair that is comfortable for you and allows you to sit upright. When sitting, think about the following aspects of good posture:

It's important to keep your spine straight and relaxed.

Avoid slouching because your heart is closed off when you're slumped over. During meditation, you'll want to keep your heart and mind open.

Your shoulders should be relaxed, but slightly rolled back and down.

Hands should be placed on your lap, on the arms of a chair, or on a cushion.

The back of your neck should feel long and loose, and your head should be straight with your chin slightly tucked in.

Your jaw and face should be relaxed. Your feet should be flat on the ground. Meditation chairs designed specifically for sitting comfortably and achieving optimal posture are available. To see what's available, do a Google search for "meditation chairs."

After a heavy meal, avoid meditating.

According to research, when the body is digesting food, mental activity increases. Avoid doing your meditation right after a large meal to avoid unnecessary noise in your mind.

After meditation, don't rush out.

Sit quietly for a few minutes longer after you've finished your meditation. This is a good time to reflect on and assimilate your experience. Be aware of any hunches or revelations you may have.

This allows you to fully immerse yourself in your meditative state. It also serves as a portal for integrating this experience into your'real world,' rather than keeping it separate from your daily routine. Your'real self' will begin to guide you daily as you learn to listen to your inner voice.

Make it a daily habit to meditate.

Meditation has a cumulative effect on your health. This means that as you meditate on a regular basis, you will reap an increasing number of benefits.

Make meditation a part of your daily routine by meditating at least once or twice a day if you're serious about improving yourself through meditation. With commitment and consistency, the rewards you receive will grow.

Step 2: Decide on a meditative posture.

It is not necessary to sit on a cushion and cross your legs. Because it is a traditional way of sitting, many Asians do so. Chairs belonged to kings, not to commoners. Despite the fact that times have changed, many Asians still prefer to sit on the ground. If you don't want to sit with your legs crossed, don't worry about it.

It'll suffice to use a stool or a chair without a back. Because constantly orienting yourself to sit upright can mean the difference between falling asleep and staying awake, you'll need one without a back.

The meditation session also includes continuously balancing yourself, but we'll get to that later. If you want to meditate while commuting, make an effort to stay awake, alert, and with your spine straight.

Make an effort to wiggle your butt out behind you, regardless of where you sit. This position not only forces you to lean back to avoid falling forward, but it also prevents you from sitting on your tailbones, or coccyx, at the end of your spine. Even with a cushion beneath you, this can begin to hurt, or it can lead to coccygodynia, a painful condition. You want to feel grounded as you sit firmly on the ischial tuberosities, whether you're sitting cross-legged or on a stool (also known as the sitting or sit bones). The bottom of the hipbones in the pelvis contains these. The flesh of the buttocks, or butt cheeks, usually covers these rounded bones, so most people aren't aware of them.

Lean back slightly, your spine forming an arch. This arch should support your shoulders, allowing your chest to protrude slightly. Experiment with different positions until you find one that you can comfortably hold for a few minutes.

Either fold your hands over your groin or place them on your lap. Allowing your arms to dangle at your sides will pull your shoulders down and cause soreness. Find the position that feels the most natural to you once more.

Maintain a flat foot on the ground if you're sitting on a stool. Crossing your ankles or resting one leg on top of the other is not a good idea. The weight of one leg pressing against the other will eventually cut off circulation, causing the leg to sleep or become sore.

If you want to sit cross-legged, make sure your upper leg is above the ankle bone, just beneath your calf. Placing one ankle bone directly on top of the other will eventually result in lower-ankle pain.

The general rule is that if one side of your body feels more pressure than the other, you're not balanced. Experiment with different postures until you find one that ensures that both sides are equally weighted. The more balanced you are, the more at ease you will be, and the less likely you will become numb or sleepy in some part of your body.

It's important to keep your head up. The airflow through your throat will be restricted if you tilt it too far back or forward. Allow your jaw to sag a little so that your upper and lower teeth are separated, but keep your lips closed.

Step 3: Reach a Meditative State

Mindfulness is a state where you are aware of the present moment and not recalling the past or thinking about what might happen in the future. You are right here, right now, without anything going on in your mind except whatever you are experiencing through your senses.

To be mindful is to notice what is happening in the present. There aren't any limits to keep in mind. Whatever happens within the realm of our sensory perception can be part of the mindful observation of the present. There is no winning or losing this game, just observing with our full attention, our whole being.

Negative or positive emotions, noise, temperature, textures, taste, anything seen with your eyes... all of these are all part of what we observe in mindfulness.

There is no real fixed location upon which the focus should remain. When truly mindful, you watch things simply happen. Attention shifts from here to there, fluidly and without intention or conscious direction. In mindfulness, your attention flows right along with the sensation of activities taking place.

In true mindfulness, there is no attachment to a specific outcome. To attach to or pursue a particular result would be to take the future into account. Observing something happening, we just watch and take it in. We don't judge any experience as good or bad. We don't try to avoid distractions. It's all fair game, and we watch as it plays out. We are non-participatory observers in some cases. In others, we are the ones performing the activity, and we are well within the focus of our mindfulness.

In meditation, the goal is the focus and concentration of the mind on a tiny point of sensation. It is not so with mindfulness. Focus cannot be forced within mindfulness. It's more like you are open to changes in the focus of your attention. You are not directing it. It is rather like watching it all unfold, as a passive member of the audience. Attaching to the idea that you must focus on something, in particular, will pull you out of mindfulness, and you will miss out on the full experience.

Though you might only be capable of a minute of mindfulness today, with practice, you can extend it substantially.

Mindfulness happens without selfish motives. It happens without "you," and yet you must usually make a decision for it to start.

To get an idea right now what mindfulness is – just a glimpse - think about the last time you were in a state of flow. Think of being so involved in something that you had no other thoughts besides the activity taking place and your total awareness of it. Riding a bicycle in a zig-zag or serpentine pattern through orange traffic cones on the ground requires you to be present in the moment. This sort of mindfulness arises with its own spontaneity. Your mind knows there is no room for thoughts of the past or the future, and so it just observes with the senses what the body

is doing, making minimal adjustments. You don't think about yourself during the event. You don't think about anything except what you are doing. You can't. You might hit the cones if you take your mind off of the task and out of the moment.

Mindfulness happens naturally and spontaneously but usually for very short durations. It is part of a healthy, functioning mind. What you will find out as you practice it more is that your mind becomes healthier and more alert.

Practicing mindfulness leads to wisdom about who you are and how you act and react to all sorts of challenges in your environment.

There is no real directed aim to mindfulness. The only goal is to practice it when you can. Initially, you might find yourself being mindful only a couple of times each day for a handful of seconds at a time. Later, seconds can turn into minutes and maybe even hours. We shouldn't have preconceived ideas about what will be learned or gained, but inevitably we learn something about ourselves during periods of mindfulness.

Chapter Two

Concentration in Mindfulness Vs. C oncentration in Meditation

Mindfulness seems to be highly significant in terms of aiding our meditation practice.

Meditation and mindfulness may seem to be the same thing. It is not the same, despite its resemblance. The commonality is in the emphasis on the present. We don't think about the past or the future while we meditate or practice mindfulness. We are entirely focused on the current moment.

When I initially sit down to meditate, I enjoy a few minutes of awareness. It assists me in gradually shifting my concentration from the outside world to myself, eventually limiting it down to a single concentrate on feeling my breath travel through my nostrils.

Is it the same thing as mindfulness if you concentrate on your breathing during seated meditation or on the rising and falling of your belly, or whatever you choose to focus your attention on when you meditate?

No, not at all. When we concentrate on the virtually undetectable sensation created by the breath, we call it meditation. It's not a macro-focus, but rather a micro-focus. It's a fraction of the awareness we experience when we practice mindfulness. When we meditate, it is exclusive of all other stimuli, unlike awareness, which is inclusive.

Our mindfulness attention might be on an item, a process, or an action. We may concentrate on a single task, such as eating, taking out the garbage, cleaning the dishes, washing the vehicle, bathing, repairing a bicycle, or whatever else we are doing. Mindfulness usually entails comprehensive awareness of a variety of stimuli.

Mindfulness is comparable to meditation, except it focuses on a broader range of issues. You're not gazing at a fleeting sensation that comes and goes (the breath). You're looking at everything that's going on more broadly and remaining with it, rather than allowing your thoughts to lead you into the past, present, or some fantasy.

Meditation requires a laser-like concentration on a single, distinct experience. As you inhale and exhale, your intense concentration might be on the feeling of air passing through your nose or past your top lip. Meditation entails repeatedly directing the mind's attention on this little place, thousands of times. Meditation is also known as monkey mind training or puppy training.

You're just viewing the dog with mindfulness, not instructing it in any way. Acting, judging, or changing anything requires a deliberate mental action. There is no direct action you can do right now to modify what is happening in order to achieve a desired result.

Non-interfering, non-judgmental observation is what mindfulness is all about. Meditation involves pushing and guiding the mind's concentration to adhere to a certain habit.

As a result, although the two are comparable, they are also highly distinct. The following are some similarities between mindfulness and meditation:

You've narrowed your attention to sensory input.

Your thoughts aren't stuck in the present or in the past. It's right now, right now.

There isn't much thinking going on (at least, that's the objective). The Differences Between Mindfulness and Meditation:

You concentrate on a variety of sensory things or stimuli while you practice mindfulness. There is just one feeling in meditation: the sensation of breath on a tiny region of and around the nose.

Mindfulness is something that may be done at any moment. It's possible to do it while driving, exercising, doing chores, eating, or doing almost anything else.

The Process From Within

When fresh stimuli reach the mind via one of the sense organs, we experience mindfulness. As you stand at the front entrance, your eyes shift to view and fix on a familiar bird, a sparrow, landing on the porch railing. Your mind says "bird" and then maybe narrows it down to a brown bird or a sparrow. Your mind is a master at categorizing everything it sees. It categorizes things so it can quickly make sense of them and retrieve information about a sensory item from your memory to tell you whether it's harmful or relevant to what you're experiencing right now.

That short instant when the eyes see the bird land and the mind recognizes it as a bird is a time of attention that occurs with everything that enters via the senses. The identification process in the mind occurs relatively fast with stimuli that are simple to categorise, such as those we've seen previously. Instantly, almost.

What happens when you're confronted with novel stimuli, such as a sparrow with an eighteen-inch snake tail swooping down on the fence in front of you? In this instance, our minds would have a hard time figuring out what it was. The mind would insist on a precise classification, but it would most likely settle for calling it a long-tailed bird. Perhaps a mutant bird, resulting from a strange collection of genes.

Have you ever had a peculiar sensation when you see something that perplexes you? That is the definition of mindfulness. This is a mental condition in which you are unable to put words to what you are witnessing. It's come to a halt. It's completely silent here. It's looking for a name, a reason, but there's none. This is a brand-new item. When you see something new for the first time, you experience a state of natural attentiveness or childlike wonder. You're looking at something for the first time, and you're in a different frame of mind because cognition, which relies on memory, can't figure it out. This is a kind of awareness that happens before you even think about it.

Without thinking about it, mindfulness occurs. It happens when the brain detects new inputs - before the naming process and all subsequent cognition. Thoughts, ideas, and views all occur after the naming process, therefore being attentive doesn't need them. You're not in real awareness if you're feeling one of these.

"The word is not the thing," used to remark Jiddu Krishnamurti, one of my favorite Eastern thinkers. The term comes after the item, which is what he was referring to. When we see a lovely little bird arrive on our doorstep, our minds take the magnificence of that small flying creature and turn it into a four-letter phrase that takes away so much of what it really is. The object isn't called a bird. It gives us very little information about the object we're looking at. The term is just a classification term for a feathered flying animal. The true meaning of the term 'bird' is vast. Mindfulness helps us to appreciate the beauty and wonder of the world without labels or cognition - a kind of awe. It's been likened to viewing the world through the eyes of a toddler by others. Why? When a child sees something but lacks the tools to give it a name, the child simply experiences it. It's like that with true mindfulness.

Before the judging process begins, mindfulness is being aware of what is going on in our surroundings. Things we experience via our senses are labeled and judged by the brain.

We are giving our thoughts a rest when we are aware. Every ounce of input that comes in via the eyes, ears, nose, mouth, and sense of touch is putting a halt to the lengthy process our brains desire to start.

This is something we can expand on. We may be attentive of our emotional states, as well as anything else is going on within our heads. When seen through the lens of mindfulness, anything we're going through is just observed and registered, without approval, rejection, or thinking.

Whatever our thoughts are going through might be seen as a new life experience, a new potential in the world of human existence.

Both positive and negative events are seen objectively. Without being offended. Without assigning a positive or negative value to your experience.

It is what it is, and it is not what it is not what it is not what it is

When you are attentive, you are not attempting to have more positive experiences than negative experiences. You're not focusing your thoughts on the positive and ignoring the unpleasant. Everything is happening right now for you.

Stimuli, emotions, ideas, and experiences all have equal weight in mindfulness. None of them are more or less valuable than the others. When you're attentive, you're an unbiased observer who isn't biased for or against anything. It's a calm and receptive state of mind.

It's as if you're experiencing something for the first time when you're aware.

One night, while standing chest-high in the water and resting on the wall of my apartment complex's swimming pool, I had my first encounter with mindfulness. Lights were put under the river and reflected in the rushing water, making for some fascinating reflections. The water was bouncing about in the pool as I completed swimming laps back and forth, filling it with a spectacular mix of curved and straight light reflections.

I concentrated on relaxing and took a few deep, steady breaths. I was admiring the light refractions in the water's waves. I was first attempting to grasp them with my intellect and make sense of them. I was attempting to predict what the pattern would be in the following split second, or to hold onto anything from the experience that my mind could label and therefore feel more at ease.

My brain must have finally concluded that it was an impossible feat after over a minute of attempting it. The lights, whether they were reflecting off the bouncing waves, beneath the water, or on top of the water, were all random and entirely unpredictable. Unpredictable.

Then I simply sat back and enjoyed the light display, just watching them. Following that, I had a mental change. I got completely engrossed in the present moment, as if I were seeing the whole event for the first time. My intellect had given up on attempting to categorize what was going on. It began to seem to my mind as a pure, immediate sensation. That was it. My intellect had seen what was going on. It didn't go much deeper than that. It was as if time had come to a halt, and I was trapped in a timeless dimension's space warp. It was as if I was looking at everything through the eyes of a toddler. It was both a thrilling and perplexing adventure.

It's almost as if you've been transported to another world when it happens spontaneously like way. The passage of time seems to pause. It's such a unique way of seeing and feeling the world that it's difficult to describe.

Because words aren't the thing, it's difficult to describe mindfulness using words.

It's simple, yet we often ignore it as our minds rush to label our sensations. Realizing it requires a fresh perspective. It requires additional work to notice it and realize that we are feeling it, as well as to maintain that condition while turning off the mind's need to label (name) every new input.

Step 4: Get past some of the most common stumbling blocks

Despite the fact that meditation has several advantages, many individuals do not meditate on a daily basis. Meditation's most typical obstacles are:

Lack of time due to busyness

If you say you don't have enough time to meditate, it usually implies you haven't prioritized it. Make time for meditation if you are serious about making it a part of your life. Here are a few ideas.

Don't assume it will take a long time.

Remember that regular meditation, even if performed for just five minutes a day, may have a significant and good influence on both your inner and outward lives. It will aid in the clarity and concentration of your energies. Your productivity and effectiveness will grow as a result of working with clarity and concentration, allowing you to do more in a day.

Meditation encourages people to meditate.

"The more we meditate, the more we wish to meditate," Paramahansa Yogananda, an Indian yogi and master, stated. Getting started is often all that's required. You'll want to do it again and again once you get started.

Use your imagination to come up with new ways to meditate at different times and locations.

Stop, calm your thoughts, and be attentive of the present moment while you go about your regular tasks. Begin with one-minute intervals and work your way up.

Take a minute to observe your breathing while waiting for an appointment or in line at the grocery store. Concentrate on each breath until you feel calm and comfortable.

I can't sit still due to mental chatter

Sitting may seem to be an easy task, but it is not. You feel hungry or thirsty just as you sit down to meditate, or you get an itch that won't go away, or your mind begins racing with thoughts about what you need to do or who you need to contact right when you sit down to meditate.

It is, nevertheless, possible to quiet your thoughts and stay calm. Here are some ideas:

Push yourself to overcome your apprehension.

Recognize that sitting still requires practice. Recognize that you must teach your body to be calm and silent.

Keep in mind that everything will be OK.

You'll be able to detect, accept, and let go of your mental chatter as you practice meditation. You will eventually master the art of being calm and silent. Meditation will become a source of calm, tranquility, and serenity for you.

Make an effort to concentrate your attention.

You'll have to coax your mind into doing what you want at first. Your mind is like an unruly, disobedient kid that does anything it wants until it is disciplined. It will fight the new habit you're instilling in it.

Your mind will eventually act in accordance with your commands. To concentrate your attention and bring it back to where you want it to be, use techniques like chanting, prayer, and breathing exercises.

I'm drifting off

You may be inspired to meditate, but you may fall asleep soon after you begin. At first, this is typical. You may, however, fight this in a variety of ways.

Choose a suitable meditation time.

When you feel refreshed and fully awake, the optimal time to meditate is 15 minutes to half an hour after awakening.

Meditation throughout the middle of the day is also effective. Avoid meditating too close to bedtime.

Make use of your vision.

"Close your eyes numerous times, then open them wide and gaze straight ahead," Paramahansa Yogananda said. Once or twice more, repeat the exercise. Sleepiness will no longer be a problem if you do this." During meditation, keeping your eyes up helps you remain aware and tuned in to a higher level of consciousness.

Discouragement

It takes a lot of practice to be a good meditator. Nobody expects to be able to master the piano on their first try. Meditation works the same way. It is a lengthy process.

"The most difficult, but gratifying work that we will ever do," the Buddha remarked. The good news is that every endeavor toward inner peace contributes to our long-term transformation."

Boredom

Every day, we are stimulated by a plethora of trinkets, devices, and media in modern society. It's no surprise that meditation might appear monotonous when surrounded by so many stimuli.

You'll simply have to believe that going to that place will be well worth the effort until you gain an appreciation for the beauty of inner solitude.

Having difficulty meditating

Meditation is often made more difficult than it needs to be. Being present in the moment is all that meditation entails. You can meditate if you can sit comfortably and breathe.

Sitting still, allowing yourself to be comfortable with just being, and calming your mind are the only objectives of simple mindfulness meditation. Our upbringing has instilled in us the belief that there must be a right and wrong way to do things. This erroneous belief is refuted by meditation. It's enough that you take a seat and relax in your own unique way.

Chapter Three

Improve your breathing technique

Step 5:

Take a deep breath in, hold it for a few seconds, and then slowly exhale. Was it difficult to complete? Most people are unlikely to agree. However, there is a proper way to do this that will provide the greatest benefit, and we will discuss some of those techniques in this chapter.

We don't want to fall asleep, but we also don't want to be in a relaxed state. Some techniques have the unfavorable effect of causing extreme sleepiness, which we want to avoid.

Pranayama is one of the most common breathing techniques taught in yoga classes. Pranayama has been translated as "control of breath," while the exact translation is "the science of breath." Pranayama means "breath or life force," and Yama means "control or to extend or draw out." The body benefits from receiving the proper flow of oxygen when and where it is needed, which is why it is frequently used in exercise routines. While there are many different types of pranayama, all of which have their origins in ancient India, we'll focus on two popular methods that have few side effects.

Dirga pranayama, or "three-part breathing," is the first. This breathing exercise is used to help the mind relax and focus on the present moment. You can do this exercise while sitting or lying down. You'll be able to feel your breath moving through your body more clearly if you do it while lying on your back.

Relax your body by closing your eyes. Begin by observing your natural breathing patterns without making any changes. If your thoughts drift away from your breathing, gently bring them back to it. Consider only your inhalation and exhalation patterns. Then gently inhale through your nose, filling your stomach with air until you feel rounded out. Then slowly exhale through your nose until your belly button feels as if it's reaching for your spine and your belly area feels empty of air. Rep this process five more times, for a total of six deep breath cycles that fill and empty your belly.

Draw in a little more air on the next inhale until your ribs feel like they've moved, then slowly exhale until you're out of air. For a total of six deep breaths, repeat this process five more times with the extra air. Now, on the next inhale, take in as much air as you can until you feel your stomach has been filled, your ribs have moved, and your upper chest has been filled (it should feel like your shoulders have risen), then slowly exhale until your belly button touches your spine. For a total of ten breaths, repeat this procedure. Return to your normal breathing if you become dizzy at any point.

It's not the goal of this exercise to make you hyperventilate and pass out; it's to help you control your breathing and relax. As your lungs expand and your body learns to relax into the exercise, this exercise should gradually become more natural.

The second type, known as sama vritti pranayama or "equal breathing," helps to calm the body and mind.

Start by closing your eyes and sitting in a comfortable position. Pay attention to your natural breathing patterns (inhaling and exhaling through your nose), but make no changes. As you inhale, begin counting. At this point, you should be on a four-count. Now exhale to the count's length. So, if your inhale count is four, your exhale count must also be four. As long as you keep both numbers the same, you can change the number to match your breathing style (remember, equal breathing). Even if your mind wanders, keep this breathing pattern going for several minutes. If your mind wanders, gently bring it back to the counting rhythm and your breathing pattern.

This is a simple but relaxing exercise.

Another Eastern breathing exercise instructs us on how to breathe more efficiently, similar to how we do when we sleep. This exercise aids our bodies in making better use of the oxygen we inhale, boosting our energy levels, improving mental capacity and clarity, and making us feel calmer. You must lie on the floor or in a bed for this exercise. Count your normal breaths through your nose for one minute once you've become relaxed. Between 15 and 25 breaths per minute will be the norm. Place a medium-sized heavy book on your lower stomach once you've calculated that number (below the belly button). Inhale deeply through your nose until the book begins to rise.

The book should return to its original starting point when you exhale through your nose. Repeat for several minutes, or until your breathing feels normal. Your breathing rate may slow down to 5 to 10 breaths per minute over time. These breaths will be deeper and more efficient, allowing more oxygen into the bloodstream and thus a calming effect.

One thing to keep in mind about breathing: cold air reduces the capacity of our lungs and their ability to transfer oxygen into our bloodstream. When breathing cold air, it is preferable to breathe through your nose so that the air can warm up before entering your lungs. If you're practicing breathing or meditation outside in the cold and can't breathe through your nose, wearing a scarf over your mouth and nose can help.

Other breathing techniques are taught in a variety of settings all over the world. If none of the above methods work for you, there are plenty more to choose from. Please be aware that some breathing techniques come with a warning for people who have high blood pressure or who have breathing problems due to asthma or COPD. Again, if you have any medical conditions, especially those that affect your breathing, consult your doctor before beginning any new routine to ensure you receive the necessary advice to safely complete this lifestyle change. Your doctor may be aware of a technique that is tailored to your needs. Your overall success in sticking to a meditation program that fits your lifestyle is more important than the techniques you use.

Step 6: Make a mental list of all the things you've been thinking about.

It's also a good idea to learn to let go of thoughts if you're used to thinking a lot during the day. Our lives are adversely affected by negative thoughts. The person who suffers the most when you hold on to your anger is you, not the one who made you angry. Most likely, this person isn't even considering the event that has upset you. If you keep playing around with negative thoughts of any kind, you empower others to control how your emotions hit you. When you're not meditating, it's far better to think positive thoughts because it helps you become a positive person and have a positive influence on the people you care about.

How, on the other hand, do you get rid of unwanted thoughts? When people first start meditating, this is a common problem.

Some people practice chanting meditation to help clear their minds. Others must learn to let go, which is the subject of this chapter.

What thoughts do you let go of without even realizing it on a regular basis? Well, thousands of thoughts occur during the course of a 24-hour period that you are probably unaware of. How much attention do you pay to the pedestrian crossing the street in front of your stopped vehicle when you're driving?

How much attention do you pay to the person driving the car next to you? We are surrounded by ephemeral things. As I previously stated, each moment of your life provides various triggers that lead to various thoughts, which may include:

Negative Neutral Positive

Because you place such a low value on neutral thoughts, it appears that when you want to meditate, you must first neutralize the thoughts that fall into the other two categories. This entails releasing them from your control. So, what's the best way to go about it? Negative thoughts do not contribute to a better quality of life. They make you think of negative things, and your mind may spend a lot of time rehashing old hurts or things said to you. These kinds of thoughts are useless. Imagine the thoughts as objects in the street that you pass while driving, and simply cut them off to let them go. Assume they're no more important than the things you're already chopping off. Consider them as pieces of paper floating down from the sky and vanishing from sight if you want to make it a fun exercise.

The most crucial aspect of it all is to turn off a natural instinct to judge. When you see something, you have a tendency to make snap judgments about it. The ability to let go will be hindered by judgment. It's difficult to step away from judgment when you think of an ex-boyfriend or ex-girlfriend because you believe you know what happened and how unreasonable the circumstances were. They did, however, get by. Unless you empower them by judging these thoughts, they aren't a part of who you are today. Allow yourself to be carried away. When you do, you will have achieved the highest level of empowerment possible, because every time you allow thoughts to persuade you in one direction or another, you are empowering those thoughts, making it nearly impossible to let go. Being able to do so will empower you in general, but it will especially help you meditate because you will be able to recognize those thoughts for what they are. They are invasions, and by letting go, you begin to free your mind in preparation for the meditation step. When people say things to you throughout the day, try it. Try dropping judgment and enabling yourself because when you do that, you tend to be more empathetic and don't say things in haste that you may regret at a later time. Distancing yourself from your thoughts will become easier if you are able to learn to let go. This is also a great exercise to use to let go of negativity and start to feel good about life.

Chapter Four

Calm Your Mind

You have learned how to breathe properly, you know how to relax the physical body and check for stored tension, you have decided when you can meditate and how long it is comfortable for you.

Even getting this far, if you have been practicing the previous steps, means you have been meditating.

Take a moment to congratulate yourself - you are doing it!

Now let's work on becoming a non-thinking meditator. This is the fun part. This is the stage where real results begin to happen.

You simply start with what you have learned in the previous steps, breathing deeply and relaxing the body as you go. Now that you have come this far, the rest of your journey is all about learning how to empty and clear the mind.

The goal of meditation practice is to create a clean slate for the mind, although I must admit it can be a bit challenging at first.

Once you achieve an empty mind, you won't even need to use the counting technique anymore. The Process for Clearing Your Mind

Prepare to peer in and focus on the mind.

Pay attention to your thoughts.

Get them to slow down.

Observe what kind of random things roll through your mind.

Watch them drift by and release each one.

Continue to let go of each thought as it comes up.

Slowly clear all thoughts from your mind.

Remember, non-thinking meditation is an exercise in 'Accomplishing Nothing,' which is actually a pretty cool activity!

Just keep telling yourself, there is nothing you need to do for the next few moments. You want your mind to be quiet, and you want your mind to stop bothering you endlessly with your mental to-do list.

The practice of letting go of your thoughts and allowing them to drift from your head will give you more control of how you use the mind in your life. You will no longer be a victim to the random, relentless, mind clutter that often traps your thinking process.

For these few precious moments of meditation, you want to detach from your world. Try not to identify with any of your thoughts or any of the roles you play in life.

Imagine yourself as a jelly-like energy blob floating in the cosmic soup!

The goal is to float, to be nothing, and to go nowhere. Don't think - because jelly blobs can't think. As part of this process, you have discovered how to turn your body into Jell-O, now you want to do the same thing with your mind.

If it takes your mind a while to unwind and you can't seem to stop thinking, that's ok, just be that jelly blob and watch the thoughts go by, don't follow them.

Monkey Mind must be avoided!

When you consider one idea, it instantly leads to another, and then another. This is known as having a monkey mind. Your mind becomes engrossed in a never-ending cycle of odd ideas.

These haphazard ideas sway in the mind's trees, bouncing about aimlessly. The majority of individuals can do this for hours and so get lost in the mental jungle. So, rather of following your ideas, let them go as they come.

You want to watch a concept enter your head and then let it go; you don't want to interact with it or give it any significance.

The ideas will eventually fade away, and you will have less of them. Don't attempt to empty your mind; instead, try to slow it down, withdraw from it, and let some emptiness emerge.

This exercise will release your soul, mind, and body.

There is no tension on the body or mind when you aren't thinking. You'll have a new lease on life. You'll soon have a calm, concentrated mind and a relaxed body.

Imagine anything like this if you're having trouble being a jelly blob floating in the cosmic soup, thinking about nothing:

It may seem impossible to clear your mind of all ideas, but all you have to do is persuade yourself that the world will go on without you for a while. Meanwhile, without any demands on it, your body will rest and renew you while your mind is vacant.

Allowing the mind to completely stop will allow clarity and creativity to emerge. The mind will be rejuvenated and far more capable of functioning after a time of nothingness.

Attention! Attention! Attention! Attention! Attention! Attention! Attention! Attention! Attention! Attention Even if it's based on nothing, it's still a start. Regardless of how hard we try, focusing on what is in front of us may be quite tough at times. However, when we're attempting to meditate, this issue might make the practice difficult. The objective is to either clear your mind of all ideas, good and bad, or to concentrate only on positive ones. It's truly that simple: when you're focused and peaceful, your life improves. When you don't have to, don't walk through life anxious and pressed. While you may feel as if there is no way out at times, there is, in fact, a way out.

With the practice of concentration and meditation, there are a few essentials to remember. The first step is to ensure that you receive enough sleep every night. Obviously, saying it is easier than doing it. We have children, we work late, and we even suffer from sleeplessness from time to time. Having a healthier sleeping cycle can help you become a more balanced person in general. To stay going and pushing through the day, some individuals rely on coffee and energy tablets; however, these aren't necessarily the greatest or healthiest options. Meditation may help you concentrate as well as boost your energy levels throughout the day.

It becomes more routine if you start meditating on a regular basis. When you make meditation a part of your regular routine, it becomes much simpler to do. The method becomes more successful the more you meditate. It's OK if you've tried meditation before and found it challenging. It takes time for us to develop the abilities we need for a successful meditation session. To attain the full benefit of meditation and the incredible things it can do for our mind, body, and soul, there are a few procedures that must be followed in order to meditate properly. As previously said, getting enough sleep might be challenging, but it is certainly possible. When we're younger, we're lucky in that we can concentrate better on less sleep. This, however, often changes as we become older. If we want to be fully effective in life after we reach adulthood, we must make it a priority to obtain enough sleep as many nights as possible. The ideal amount of sleep is between seven and eight hours every night. Keep in mind that sleeping less than or more than seven hours might be harmful to your health. For some of us, getting this done and sleeping for this long may be tough.

At night, we may be disturbed by children, snoring spouses, or other factors. It is critical for the meditation process that we get enough sleep every night.

Finding time to sleep is challenging, but if you're attempting to make up for missed sleep hours at night, you'll need to either establish a bedtime or find time during the day to nap. Make sure your sleep cycles are in sync, consistent, and effective, regardless of how you make up for it.

Another crucial part of meditation is removing distracting factors. It's all about unwinding when you meditate. Meditation allows you to achieve inner and mental serenity. It will be extremely difficult to concentrate if there are loud sounds, loud discussions, or other distractions around you. Try to remain in the zone while you're meditating. You must become unconcerned with what is going on around you. Turn off your phone, television, and any other electronic gadgets and immerse yourself in your own thoughts.

You will begin to genuinely understand yourself if you are able to shut out the world. Make a zone for yourself. Allow yourself to get immersed in the moment of meditation, not thinking about time, space, what's for dinner, or cleaning the house. We are often so preoccupied with our daily lives and routines that clearing our thoughts becomes impossible. It's difficult to let go of these ideas, even if it's just for a short time, when we're focused on life, school, our children, job, and other things that occupy our time and energy.

Meditating a few times a day is one approach to foster it. This may seem to be far-fetched, but it isn't. Meditation often takes 10-20 minutes. This does not have to take as long as it does. It becomes tough for us to comprehend when we go from one aspect of our life to another. When we leave work and immediately transition to mommy/daddy or wife/husband mode at home, for example, we may feel overwhelmed, as if the job never ends. After each daily transitional period, set aside a few minutes to meditate. During this time, you may practice short periods of meditation. Before you approach your next transitional phase, take a few minutes to leave your job persona behind, collect your thoughts, and let that portion of your day go.

Work by itself may be exhausting. We need to carve out time in our days to reflect on our workplace and anticipate what awaits us at home. You must allow yourself time to collect your thoughts and plan your future moves in between the transitional phases. Our ideas, emotions, and behaviors change as the environment changes. This period may be utilized to let go of any bad energy that has built up at work and begin the new transition with a clean slate. Try letting go of any bad energy while driving to and from work. If you're driving to work, try not to worry about the fight you had with your significant other earlier in the day or what you'll have to do when you get home. Remove any ideas from your head so that you can start your workday fresh.

While you're driving, try to think of happy and healthy locations. This is your own personal territory. Anything from a secluded island to a peaceful mountain chalet might be your zone. Visual meditation is the name given to this process. Visual meditation is defined as the ability to imagine an idea or a location and concentrate entirely on that location.

This sort of meditation works because it helps us to imagine and image what we desire in our brains. We may imagine ourselves at a place we desire to be in life or on vacation.

Make sure it's a secure and healthy environment full of peace and tranquility, whatever it is and wherever it is. Whatever your comfort zone is, make sure you can clear your thoughts while you're thinking about this stunning location.

If you can't clear your mind of everyday ideas, you'll have a hard time meditating. You'll have to practice this, and it'll take some time. Be patient; with time, you'll learn to empty your thoughts when the moment is perfect.

Working with Emotions is the eighth step.

Meditation can help you recognize that you are always thinking throughout time. Your mind bombards you with notion after thought while you move about aware throughout the day... With some of those ideas, emotions rise and fall.

Isn't it fantastic to have complete control over all of your feelings?

Examine your ability to recognize when you are furious. Because it is a strong emotion that is simple to see, anger is one of the easiest emotions to recognize and become conscious of.

When you're enraged, what happens?

There is usually an unmet expectation. You didn't obtain anything you desired, needed, or expected.

When you take away a child's sweets, she feels enraged because she expected to be able to keep eating it, and her expectation has come to an end.

Adults may feel enraged for a variety of reasons, including when the computer they're using freezes and they can't write, operate the mouse, or get to the start button to shut it off. You feel enraged because you no longer have the expectation of being able to use the computer without interruption. Expectations are just that: they are deceptions. We take them for granted, yet they are rife with inaccuracies and uncertainties.

We should not grow attached to anything, according to Buddhism, which seems to fit well with meditation and the feelings that come with it. We shouldn't become hooked to things like ideas, friends, money, computers, gadgets, documents, reading, music, CDs, watches, jewelry, or even our loved ones.

That's not to suggest we shouldn't have nice sentiments for folks we care about... but we shouldn't grow connected to them, which is a different thing.

Expectations are what attaches people... the assumption that something will keep providing us with pleasure indefinitely. It's clear that electronics and other material objects don't last forever... they become scratched, lose their color, get misplaced, lose their worth, break, and so on.

It's a little more difficult to explain why connection to individuals isn't so wonderful...

People don't always do what we want or anticipate. We like individuals because we anticipate their actions to continue to provide us joy or alleviate our suffering.

People, on the other hand, are always in flux. Consider how much one person's life may change in a lifetime! How many eighty-year-olds have been closest friends for seventy years?

To begin with, a large number of people have passed away. Second, during the course of a lifetime, they all change dramatically. Your girlfriend or boyfriend, as well as the person you know and love today, will change. It can't be helped. It is the nature of things. Meditation allows you to perceive things more clearly.

Attachment to something isn't going to make you happy... it's just going to make you unhappy for a short while. Meditation assists you in letting go of attachments... In other circumstances, the shift is abrupt and dramatic: when you become aware of the reality of those words, your connection to everything starts to fade. Everything you were once connected to becomes disillusioned with you.

Your anger and other emotions that were previously based on things for which you had high expectations will gradually fade away as well.

However, your inherent goodness remains!

If it's feasible for you to imagine, you may fall in love...
As a consequence of meditation and disenchantment, you
may achieve such equanimity that you are overflowing with
pleasure and in an unshakeable condition of calm.

Nothing has the capacity to hurt you... agony that
was previously generated by thinking... attachment. It's
a wonderful condition for which words are inadequate,
therefore I'll end here.

So, how might meditation assist you in other ways? For
starters, it's a critical component of emotional intelligence
development. You'll notice that as you get more conscious
of yourself and how you react to certain circumstances,
you'll become more aware of how others react to similar
situations. Emotional intelligence is a term used to describe
this kind of awareness, and it is now often regarded as
incredibly valuable. Indeed, some scientists are beginning to
favor assessing emotional intelligence above determining a
person's potential.

While you may question whether or not you are good enough
or clever enough on a regular basis, chances are you do not
question whether or not you are compassionate or a good
listener. If you've ever seen The Big Bang Theory, you'll know
that the protagonist, Sheldon Cooper, is shown as a person
with a high IQ but a low EQ factor. This has an influence on his

professional and personal development in coming seasons. This is a very regular occurrence: no matter how intelligent you are, you will need a certain level of emotional intelligence to fully flourish in life.

To determine your emotional intelligence levels, begin by asking yourself the following questions:

Do you consider yourself to be a calm individual? Are you able to keep your cool under pressure?

Are you a caring person? Do you have a good sense of what other people want?

Do you have a proclivity for making smart judgments, in your opinion?

Is it possible for you to pay attention to what others have to say? Do you think about what other people have to say?

Do you think you have a good impact on the individuals you interact with?

Do you have a tendency to act on your impulses? On a scale of one to ten, how impulsive would you rate yourself?

Do you have a cheerful or sad mindset?

Were your responses mostly negative? If you do, your EQ is probably low. The good news is that your EQ can be improved by meditation, regardless of how low it is. Meditation is known to assist you in assessing and attuning yourself to other people's emotions in addition to helping you detach from negative ideas. Poker players, for example, are recognized for having extraordinarily high levels of emotional intelligence; this superior emotional intelligence helps them to'read' emotions in their opponents, such as fear or reluctance, and hence make better decisions.

Most significantly, your emotional intelligence levels will aid you in coping with years of emotional baggage that has hampered your inner mind control. The days of being unable to regulate your emotions are long gone. You may now actively deal with your anxiety, despair, and negative thinking patterns with the aid of meditation, replacing them with strong reasoning skills and problem-solving talents.

Chapter Five

Educate yourself

So, what's the big deal about this? What exactly is it about it that makes it so popular? We've compiled a list of the top reasons to meditate for your convenience.

Meditation, for starters, aids mental training. Our minds do a lot of drifting and thinking throughout our days and throughout our lives. It could be that job interview you didn't get, a test you failed, or the house you want to buy next week. Whatever it is, meditation can help you relax and focus on the present moment by removing stress, worry, and anxiety. We can achieve clarity, serenity, and compassion as a result of this practice. As a result, we and anyone who comes into contact with us are affected. We can effectively combat our worries by gaining a better understanding of our breathing, thoughts, and emotions.

Second, meditation will assist you in your quest for self-awareness. Rather than flushing your mind and thoughts or husheing your emotions, meditation helps you pay attention without becoming lost in them, contrary to popular belief. Mindfulness meditation is a type of meditation that helps people focus on what's going on in the present moment. It encourages you to pay attention to and listen to your thoughts and emotions without putting yourself down or praising yourself. It's not as simple as it appears. The practice is simple, so that's an advantage. However, mastering this practice takes time and a lot of practice because you have to get it under control and in order before you can reap the benefits. As a result, focusing on the present moment rather than drifting or daydreaming aids in improving our control over our actions. Even in the most infuriating situations, this exercise helps to create space for compassion, tolerance, and endurance. We can discover the source of our misery and find ways to alleviate it with continued training.

Third, meditation is like going on a journey to discover who you are. We understand that your thoughts might wander. We won't be able to make you stop thinking because that would be tantamount to killing you. Meditation allows you to be conscious of your thoughts rather than shutting them out. However, you must not overthink it or assign a positive or negative value to it. It's just a thought, and it needs to be recognized as such. So, how do we proceed? You get up and leave. You then return your focus to your breathing and the present moment.

For many people, meditation is a multifaceted concept. As a result, attempting to define and define it is restricted. It's best if you go into this activity with an open mind and don't overthink it.

Step ten: Determine your focal point

You focus on one thing at a time in concentration meditation, which can be your breath, an image of something that calms you, a soothing sound, or even an object like a candle flame. One of the reasons I recommended having candles in your meditation space is for this reason. What good does it do? Focusing on just one thing, on the other hand, improves your ability to concentrate and reduces your proclivity to be distracted by objects or situations. You must try to get used to a specific way of concentrating. It's not like when you're focused on learning or reading a specific book. You aren't attempting to enter data. Instead, it could be described as a stare or focus on resisting the urge to think or look at something else.

Unnecessary distractions, such as past or future thoughts or worries, can cause anxiety or stress. When you practice concentration meditation and master the skill of focusing on one thing at a time, you can reduce stress by focusing solely on the actions you need to take to relieve it. Believe it or not, when you practice this type of meditation, you let go of worldly thoughts, which benefits your subconscious mind by giving it a break from all of the stimulation to which it has become accustomed.

So, how should you go about practicing concentration meditation in order to alleviate stress and anxiety? Next, we'll talk about:

Concentration Meditation: How to Do It

The steps to concentration meditation are as follows:

Find a Relaxing Spot: To begin, find a quiet place to meditate where no one can bother you; this could be your room or a spot in your backyard under a tree. Make sure you're free of distractions by turning off your phone and turning off any noisy appliances when you're sitting in your meditation spot. You will be able to meditate more successfully if you can get away from the ringing of the phone and the noise of the world in general.

Relax: Once you've found a comfortable spot to meditate, sit cross-legged, sit on the couch, or lie down on the couch - whatever position makes you feel most at ease. Whatever position you choose, the most important thing is to keep your back straight. If you sit on the ground under a tree, I recommend bending your knees and crossing your ankles for people who are new to meditation.

Tip 1: dim the lights and light some candles if you're sitting inside. Why is it necessary for you to do so? Lighting candles, on the other hand, creates a relaxing atmosphere, making it easier to meditate. If lighting candles isn't your thing, hang an image of something that calms you on the wall to meditate in front of. Keep the lighting dim so you don't get distracted from your work.

Tip 2: set a timer: the goal of meditation is to improve your focus, which can be undermined if you are constantly distracted by the clock. Make a timer so you don't have to look at your watch to see what time it is. Keep your meditation sessions brief at first and gradually increase them as you gain experience. Because the "tick, tick" of a timer can distract you, you should use one that does not tick.

5-10 minute sessions work best at the start, and you can have these sessions twice a day. Once you get used to it, increase the time of sessions to get better results. I always suggest to beginners that they use 15 minutes as the time to put aside for meditation. That gives you enough time to set yourself up and also to write in your journal after you have finished meditating while your heartbeat and blood pressure get back to normal.

Focus on One Thing: Once you are through the aforementioned steps, take a deep breath, and focus on one thing. For this example, I am considering that you are focusing on an image you placed in front of you, the flame of the candle you lit, or just your breath - it's entirely up to you.

Start noticing the detailing of the image. For instance, if it's an image of a cow grazing in a field, then focus on each detail of the image. What color is the cow? How many spots does the cow have? Etc. If you have decided to use a candle, then concentrate on the flicker of the candle and relax into your concentration so that you are breathing deeply and not really taking notice of anything except the flame of the candle. If you decide to concentrate on your breath, then breathe into the count of 8 and breathe out to the count of ten and keep the rhythm of your breathing constant. You are not accustomed to breathing this deeply, and this is what puts you in a relaxing state.

Step 11: Find Compassion

Self-compassion is of tremendous importance when making a difficult life change in your life, such as healing from trauma. Self-love will help you overcome challenges that may seem impossible. It involves the repetition of specific phrases that shift the attention from judgment, dislike, and ridicule, to caring, love, and understanding.

In this meditation practice, the instructor will ask you to come up with thoughts and memories when you felt love for yourself, care, happiness, and contentment. The instructor will also ask you to imagine sending thoughts of love, peace, and affection to the people dearest to you.

Assume that with every breath you inhale love from them, and exhale love and affection back to them.

You probably have memories of childhood and may well have been told to mind your manners and be mindful of how you behave. Mindfulness extends a little further than that, and many adults don't feel mindful as they go through their everyday chores or things that they have to do. Basically, this means being in the moment that you are living. The best way to describe mindfulness is being aware of all of your senses. If you take a walk in the garden in the early morning, you will be able to use mindfulness to really enjoy the experience. Wrap up warm, take a stroll, and you will probably see many things you have never seen before because you haven't really looked. What about the cobwebs that have been spun overnight? Did you see them and the dew drops that hang from them and look like jewels? Did you notice that?

Mindfulness means using every sense that you have, and if you incorporate this into your life, you are embracing all the opportunities that come your way and making the most of them. That's very important to people who meditate. To be present in the breath is something that doesn't come naturally to people whose worlds are filled with chaos. Thus, sometimes you need to step back and use the senses that you were given when you were born and feel the earth around you, hear the noises of nature, touch the textures and taste the flavors of life. Being mindful really does go hand in hand with meditational practice. It means stilling yourself at this very moment. Whether you are simply observing the world or drinking a cup of coffee, mindfulness makes that small experience into a real experience. You may be wondering what I mean by that, but how often have you eaten your sandwiches without really noticing the taste of what you are eating?

The trouble with this world of overload is that we are encouraged by our peers and by advertisements to get things done and do them quickly, and thus, we lose the ability to use our senses in the way that they were intended to be used.

When you are mindful, you are completely absorbed in the moment. You may be cleaning floors, but if you are, your attention will be on every detail of cleaning that floor. Although this may seem a very banal task, it's as important as everything else that you do if you do it intentionally and pay attention to each detail, instead of allowing yourself to be interrupted and finding no joy in the job at all.

Chapter Six

Make Meditation a Daily Routine

You can supplement your sitting meditation by spending a few minutes each day being aware of what you're doing.

When you eat, for example, pay attention to the first three bites. Don't talk to others, respond to that text message, or look around you. Really notice your food. What are its flavors? What textures does it possess? What is its temperature like? How does it smell? How does it feel when it touches your lips? When it enters your mouth? When you chew on it? When it goes down your throat?

Do the same for your drink.

When you walk, pay attention to the first three steps. How do your feet feel in your shoes? How does the ground feel? Is it hard or yielding? What's the temperature around you? Is there a breeze? How do your clothes feel as they rub against your body? What are you hearing?

You can then let your mind get back into automatic mode.

If you practice long enough, however, your mind becomes more and more conscious of what's happening around you. You become more sensitive to things, sensations, feelings, and phenomenon, but your emotional reaction to them becomes less.

If you miss a sitting meditation session, try to make up for that loss by prolonging your active meditation practice. Rather than really paying attention to the first three bites of your food, the first three gulps of your drink, or the first three steps of your walk, focus on the entire session.

The next time you find yourself in a stressful situation like a test, meeting, or argument, use active meditation. Pay attention to your physical sensations and emotional reactions.

Locate your discomfort. Is your heart beating faster? Are your hands clenching up into fists? Are you sweating? If so, how much and how little? Where are you sweating? Are you sweating more in some parts and less in others?

Are you embarrassed? Scared? Tense? All emotional reactions have a physical counterpart. Is your chest tingling? Is your throat tightening up? Is your jaw hurting because of clenched teeth?

Don't run away from your discomfort. Treat it as you would itchiness during sitting meditation. Focus on it, locate it, and determine how strong or weak it is. The more you can focus your mind on pain and discomfort, the more you can detach yourself from it, and the better you'll be at dealing with it.

Part 2: Relax - Effective Relaxation Techniques

Abdominal Breathing for Quick Relaxation

By now, you likely recognize the benefits of deep breathing and understand that it can have a profound effect on your body and your emotional makeup. Putting it into practice should be a part of your daily meditation. Even a few moments of deep breathing and meditation can help to bring you back into focus, reduce your anxiety levels, and provide you with inner energy and strength.

Many people who recognize the benefits of deep breathing exercises schedule them throughout the day. You can set a reminder on your cell phone or perhaps on your computer, which will help you to remember to put them into practice. Here are a few of those techniques that can change your life for the better.

Cleansing Breath - A simple cleansing breath can have a profound effect on you when it is done at the right time. Many forms of meditation start with a cleansing breath, which helps to open the airways and allows you to breathe normally. As you experience stress through the day, it can limit your breathing and cause you to breathe shallowly. This reduces your blood oxygen levels and contributes to the tension that you are experiencing. When you recognize that you are tense, you can use a cleansing breath to bring your body and mind back into focus. The true benefit of a cleansing breath is the fact that it can be done at any time and takes no time to do. In fact, you can even do a deep breath in the middle of a presentation to help yourself focus and give you the strength to go on.

The basics of taking a cleansing breath are to breathe deeply as if you were breathing the air into your belly. This deep breathing allows the oxygen to get deep into your lungs, including the lower lobes, which are often untouched because of shallow breathing practices. As you breathe out, allow your abdomen to collapse and sink back into the area of your spinal column. During this breath, pay close attention to your ribs. Your ribs should expand and contract significantly, each time that you take a cleansing breath. Inhale to the count of four and exhale to the count of four. A simple cleansing breath can help to clear the mind and refresh the body.

Technique 1, Square Breathing - This is one of the easier deep breathing techniques to master. It only takes a few moments to do, but the effects of doing so can be profound. This is not only a technique that is known among naturalists or those who are familiar with meditative practices; it is also scientifically known and widely recommended by psychologists and psychiatrists for calming the mind. There is scientific evidence that square breathing can change the balance of oxygen and carbon dioxide in the body. It helps to relax the mind while at the same time providing energy for the tired soul. Here are the four steps of square breathing.

Breathe in - During the first step, you will close your eyes (if possible) and relax your mind. Throughout the process, you will focus entirely on your breathing. The first step is to breathe in through your nose to the count of four. Fill your lungs to a comfortable level, and be sure that you are breathing deeply.

Hold - The second step of the process of square breathing is to hold your breath to the same count of four.

Breathe out - You will now exhale through the mouth quietly to the count of four. Try to maintain the same pace as your counting. Do not force the air out of your lungs; allow it to happen naturally.

Hold - The final step in the process is to allow your lungs to remain empty for the same count of four.

Repeat this process four times, and you will feel the difference in your mental clarity, energy levels, and stress levels. If it is difficult for you to maintain this exercise to the count of four in any of its parts, you can reduce the count to three. It is better to reduce the count than to go quickly to the count of four.

Technique 2, The Stimulating Breath - Adopted from a yoga technique, the stimulating breath is designed to increase your alertness and to provide energy to the body. It is something that you can do throughout the day to give yourself the mental and physical boost that you need to continue in today's stressful world. When it is done correctly, it can give you a similar feeling to the heightened awareness you experience after a workout. The effort put into the stimulating breath can be felt in the diaphragm, the abdomen, the chest, and the back of the neck. It has been likened to a natural cup of coffee. You should be aware that this breathing exercise can be quite noisy, so it may not be appropriate for all situations.

Keep your mouth closed during this exercise, but do not purse your lips. Inhale and exhale through your nose rapidly, trying to keep the breaths even and short.

The timing of your breath should be in a cycle, with three breaths in and out every second. This exercise is sometimes called the bellows because of the movement to the diaphragm. When you complete the cycle of three breaths in and out, take a normal breath.

Continue to repeat the cycle, followed by a single, normal breath. When you first start, you should limit the duration of the exercise to a maximum of 15 seconds. That will keep you from hyperventilating, which will have the opposite effect of what you are trying to achieve. As you grow accustomed to using the stimulating breath technique, you can increase the length gradually until a full minute is achieved.

Technique 3, Breath Counting - This type of breathing technique can be used as a precursor to the 4-7-8 breathing exercise, which we will discuss next. It helps you to get a feel for counting your breath, and although it is simple, this breathing exercise can have a profound effect on the mind and body.

During the breath counting exercise, pay careful attention to your posture and try to get into a position that is comfortable. Close your eyes, and start with a cleansing breath. From that point, continue to take several deep, even breaths. Do not try to force this part of the exercise or any part of the breath counting technique. It should occur naturally, and it is a quiet exercise, so it can be done in any location.

Each phase of this exercise should begin with a deep, comfortable breath. When you exhale the first time, count quietly in your mind to one.

With the second breath, slow your exhale to the count of two and continue to increase the exhale time until you are counting to five. That is considered to be a single cycle.

Continue immediately after finishing one cycle to begin a new cycle, where you will breathe in deeply and exhale to the count progressively, starting with one. You can continue this meditative

exercise for ten minutes, and you should feel the effects of it on your mind and body.

Technique 4, the 4-7-8 Exercise - This exercise is sometimes referred to as the relaxing breath, and when you begin to incorporate it into your meditative practices, you will see that it has earned its reputation. It is a simple exercise that can be done in any position and any location, and it is quiet enough that you can do it at work, in line at the grocery store, or even when you are sitting at a red light. This technique is very similar to square breathing, but the count is different, and you may find that it is a more in-depth exercise that can have a more profound effect.

During the time that you are doing the relaxing breath exercise, the tip of the tongue should be pressed against the roof of the mouth immediately behind the upper front teeth. When you are exhaling, it will be done through the mouth, and the air should go around the tongue. If this produces an abnormal sensation, slightly purse your lips, but otherwise, keep your lips relaxed.

During the first step of the 4-7-8 breathing exercise, you will exhale through your mouth, around your tongue, as was described above. This may make a slight sound, but if you are in a public location, modify the breath to remain quiet and avoid embarrassment.

After emptying your lungs, close your mouth and inhale through the nose while counting to four at a comfortable pace.

You will hold your breath, now that your lungs are full, to the count of seven. Maintain the same pace during the time that you are counting.

Exhale your breath through your mouth and around your tongue to the count of eight. Continue to maintain the same pace while counting.

Those steps together make a single cycle. You should immediately start with a new cycle until you complete a total of four cycles.

In a similar way to square breathing, the relaxed breath technique acts as a tranquilizer for the body. It helps to calm the nervous system naturally and can be done at any time of the day, as frequently as you need in order to experience the benefits.

As you continue to use these breathing techniques, you will become efficient at doing them and will continue to experience additional benefits. You can also modify these techniques to a certain extent and even incorporate all of them throughout the day. You will find that they provide you with a short duration of meditation that can help you to deal with the stress of life and allow you to be relaxed in your mind but have energy as well.

CPSIA information can be obtained
at www.ICGtesting.com
Printed in the USA
BVHW060412110522
636630BV00007B/570